D1279685

ISAAC MURPHY

I Dedicate This Ride

BOOKS BY FRANK X WALKER

Affrilachia
Buffalo Dance: The Journey of York
Black Box
When Winter Come: The Ascension of York

ISAAC MURPHY

I Dedicate This Ride

poems by

FRANK X WALKER

OLD COVE PRESS

LEXINGTON, KENTUCKY 2010

Published by
OLD COVE PRESS
P. O. Box 22886
Lexington, Kentucky 40522
www.oldcove.com

Old Cove Press
PUBLISHERS/EDITORS: Nyoka Hawkins, Gurney Norman

Composed in Minion
Prepress services: Beau Graphics, Lexington KY
Printed through Four Colour Print Group, Louisville KY

Old Cove Press thanks
Aaron Anderson, Teresa Burgett, Eric Taylor and Duncan Veach

Copyright © 2010 by Frank X Walker
All rights reserved

ISBN: 978-0-96754243-0

Printed in the U.S.A.

FIRST EDITION
Second printing

Cataloging-in-publication data
Walker, Frank X, 1961-
Isaac Murphy: I dedicate this ride / poems by Frank X Walker. – 1st. ed. –
Lexington, Ky. : Old Cove Press, 2010.
88 p. ; 24 cm.
1. Murphy, Isaac Burns, 1861-1896–Poetry. 2. African-American jockeys–
Kentucky–19th century–Poetry. 3. African Americans in horse racing–
Kentucky–19th century–Poetry. I. Title. II. Title: I dedicate this ride.
ISBN 10: 0-9675424-3-X
ISBN 13: 978-0-96754243-0
PS3623.A359 I83 2010

for Lucy Murphy

Contents

Introduction

AFRICAN-AMERICAN JOCKEY ISAAC BURNS MURPHY (1861–1896) is considered by many to be the greatest jockey in the history of thoroughbred racing. The first to win the Kentucky Derby three times (1884, 1890, 1891), Murphy won an unprecedented 44% of the races he entered.

Part of the lore surrounding Murphy's legacy was his penchant for not using the whip. He preferred to ride his mounts into the winner's circle by using his well-honed skills and simply *talking* to his horses.

In Murphy's time, thoroughbred racing was dominated by African-American jockeys. In the first Kentucky Derby thirteen of the fifteen jockeys were black. Of the first twenty-eight runnings of the Derby (1875–1902), fifteen were won by African-American riders.

Murphy died of pneumonia in 1896 at the age of thirty-five. A special coffin was ordered modeled after that of Union General Ulysses S. Grant. Murphy was originally buried in the African Cemetery in Lexington, Kentucky. His grave is now at the Kentucky Horse Park. Lucy Murphy's body was left behind. Her burial site is unknown.

The poems imagined/spoken here by Isaac Murphy and his wife Lucy, his mentor Eli Jordan, and his parents James and America Burns carry Murphy's story forward. They shine a light on the life of America's most celebrated black jockey, his family and community, and the historical canvas on which his extraordinary life played out.

Murphy's Secret
Isaac Murphy

When folks find out I'm *him*
they always want to know what I say to 'em.
If they be white I tell 'em I say

'Run an run quick
or they gone feed you to the niggers.'
An they usually laugh an leave me be.

If they be black I tell 'em the truth.
I tell 'em how I cup my hand to a horse's ear
how I let it catch some wind so they remember

what it sound like to run full out,
to know you not just a field hand or a work horse
but beautiful an strong an smart.

I don't never have to ask 'em to honor somethin'
you can't really see   just feel.
I just nudge 'em like they exhausted mammas do

soon as they are born an licked dry
until they unfold them wobbly legs an stand.
When I'm up there I rub my hands against they neck

lean into they ear, pretend I'm the wind an whisper
'Find yo purpose. Find yo purpose'   an hold on.

I Dedicate This Ride
Isaac Murphy

When I come barreling down the stretch
I always think about my daddy, James Burns,
a runaway slave turned soldier.

At the start of every race I pretend
he's in the crowd, standing at attention
watching me ride for the first time,
his brass belt buckle gleaming
like his proud mouth.

I tell myself I don't dare lose,
that this race is for the Union.
For all ex-slaves who joined up,
who stole away with their families.
They taught us about sacrifice,
dug trenches, carried supplies
and ate a whole lot of rebel bullets

just so they could keep the freedom
they hungered so much for.
Just so their children could dream.

So I could ride horses and enjoy true quiet
and these visits with him
in the middle of all this noise.

I Thought Slavery Was a Song

Isaac Murphy

*I will sing unto the LORD, because he hath
dealt bountifully with me. Psalms 13:6*

I don't remember any shackles.
I remember Mamma always singing
and Daddy whistling out the door in the half-light
of morning, returning to us almost mute
after the tobacco barn swallowed the sun.

I didn't know what it meant to be *worked like a dog*
but I knew it had something to do with being
too dog-gone tired to eat at night.

I have this memory of Mamma handing me
a tied-up old rag and sending me to a field
where Daddy was plowing. He was sweating so hard
it looked like he'd been standing in the rain.

I remember how he hummed when he unwrapped
Mamma's gift biscuit and bacon scraps,
the moaning sounds he made with every slow bite
and the song on his lips when he finished.

I remember him shooing me out of the shade
he'd told me to stand in and on back to the cabin,
his clucking and chatter with the mules,
the sounds of their stubbornness and mine
but mostly   I remember the songs.

For Family and Country

James Burns

[T]he arm of the slave [is] the best defense against
the arm of the slaveholder.
—Frederick Douglass, 'Men of Color, To Arms!' 1863

In Kentucky, it was no short row
to volunteer up for the Union
even with the promise a bounty.

The first violence we met
was at the hands a hostile white farmers
an not their angry Gray army.

Around Lebanon, a white gang ripped the shirts
off a backs with a hundred lashes
to every colored man lookin' to sign up.
In Marion, some had they left ears cut off.

But it didn't stop over ten thousan' a us
from makin' our way to Camp Nelson to serve.

When they passed the law
freein' wives an children of enlisted men,
escapin' the yoke was so desirable

even hard-ankled colored women
up an married soldiers,
just to get some of that freedom for themselves.

The Right to Bear Arms

James Burns

Ten thousand of Kentucky's 23,703 black enlistees
passed through Camp Nelson during the Civil War.

If a colored man loved horses an freedom
there could be nothin' more like heaven
than to steal away to Camp Nelson by moonlight
hoping to join the Cavalry.

The camp was protected on three sides
by limestone cliffs that rose up out
the water like pearly gates.

They give us uniforms an boots an hardtack
to make us feel like soldiers. But we started out
diggin' trenches an latrines, collectin' the dead
an servin' as boys for white officers.

Our soldiers finally saw action in Lexington
an Harrodsburg, was part a Burbridge's
an Stoneman's raids into Virginia, helped capture
Saltville an destroy the saltworks there.

In a hundred an sixty-six black regiments
we had us almost a hundred black officers,
none bigger than captains,
but all a us much bigger than slaves.

Camp Nelson
America Burns

They turned slaves into soldiers
ova near Nicholasville. They built
a school an a colored hospital too.
But only after people raised a stink

an made 'em feel guilty
for turnin' alla women an chil'ren
outta camp on a cold winter night
an had so many of 'em freeze to death.

My husband signed up for the Union
an he never come back. They say
he died in camp a consumption.

I say they didn't build that hospital
fast enough.

The Heart of the Matter
America Burns

After the war, the only thing
that itched more than tastin' freedom
was reconnectin' families.

Our folk roamed the countryside
in search a relatives an friends
that might still be held in bondage.

Big mammas stepped in for missin' mammas
an daddies. Everybody went off in search a
chil'ren that had been sold off.

Wives that had been left behind
wrapped themselves around returnin' husbands,
or what was left a them that did survive.

I took my babies to the city to live wit my daddy.
I heard the county was indenturin' up
colored chil'ren to they former masters.

A slavery trick if I ever heard one.
I refuse to let my chil'ren grow up in bondage
no matter what new name they was callin' it.

The Good Book

America Burns

There was many a black church
openin' its doors
when we first come to Lex'nin.

They all offered tickets to heaven
jumped up an down in the floor
sang an moaned all day
an took our pennies.

But the ones that seemed most righteous
to me taught black folk an they chil'ren
how to scratch out they own name
wit pen an ink.

Not just in the dirt wit a stick
like I learned. They taught folk
how to find a verse in the Bible an read it,
which give 'em all a better chance

to look for God on they own—
an find them whole selves
before them close the book.

How Faith Works

America Burns

One generation out a slavery
black folk still tryin' to figure out
religion—what to call it, how to use it
an how to let it use us.

Sayin' we now free after the war
didn't fix nothin'
nor everybody that was broken
or take away our need to be prayed up.

Survivin' in this place
mean that masters become daddies,
truth become lies become laws.
Everything change   except God.

We may a forgotten the old ways
but it didn't keep Him from showin' up
every time two or more a us
got together, found our knees
an married our voices to song.

What Mamma Knows
Isaac Murphy

My daddy's joining up with the Union
earned us our freedom.
Mamma brought us all the way here
to Lexington so we could keep it.

When I helped her tote dirty laundry
from white folks' back steps
I learned that a generous smile
and good manners could get you

just as far as bowing and scraping
but with your pride still intact.
How it could snatch the nasty
right off of some folks' tongues

unless they'd already made up
their mind to all but spit on you.
When I saw Mamma heap even
more kindness on them

'til something like shame
rose in the corner of their eyes,
I made up my mind to grow up
a gentleman   to work hard,
to earn respect, to mind my tongue
and to always try to disarm ugly with a smile.

Defining Wealth

Isaac Murphy

In the years around Lexington after the war
young boys like me with the *right* attitude
might look to wait tables at a nice whites-only hotel,
work as porters, messengers, janitors or even stewards.

But a few of us were lucky enough to serve
beautiful four-legged masters instead.

We might start out mucking stalls
and work up to exercising or grooming.
But a good trainer or jockey could make
enough money to buy and race his own horses.

Now some say that's rich. But Granddaddy Murphy
taught me any man who owns himself is rich.

So down the homestretch, I feel like I own Isaac,
I own the horse, I own the race, and every time
I cross that finish line in front of all the other riders,
I even feel like I own the whole day.

Uncle Eli's Boys

Eli Jordan

African-American trainer Eli Jordan
is credited with molding the trio of black jockeys
Tom Britton, Isaac Murphy and 'Pike' Barnes.

They was just scrawny little boys
that became like sons to me.
So I set out to teach 'em everything I knew.
I trusted the horses—the real experts—
to teach 'em the rest.

Ike was my best student ever.
Never seen a boy so hungry to learn.
I say boy but he stopped bein' a boy soon as
that first horse threw him an he let go a his
fear an got right back on.

Always early to work. Spent his extra time
studyin' an askin' questions. Paid attention
to how different each horse's spirit was.
Could always tell the hot-headed sprinters
from the pack runners.

A trainer is judged by the success a his stable.
A rider is measured by his wins.
Ike got his mounts across the finish line
on his own, but he always credited
the horse, then me.

Uncle Eli's Rules
Eli Jordan

Learn your numbers an always do the math.
Don't ride a horse you don't yet know.

Don't ride a horse that don't know you neither.
Don't race a horse you ain't rode.

Don't forget it's a race an not no parade.
Only ask the horse for what you need to win.

A horse gotta run like it got blinders on—you don't.
Set the pace on the track after you set it in your heart.

Leave your fears at the starting line.
If you must be afraid, be afraid a losin'.

Temple of My Familiar
Eli Jordan

I don't call myself a religious man
but when you talk to horses an know they listenin'

when you can separate in the thick mornin' fog
the sound of a dam schoolin' her newborn
from a stallion flirtin' with a mare

when you know ain't nothin' more breathtakin'
than a new sun at daybreak but a minutes-old foal
finally findin' its legs

when you can stand in the middle of a barn
right next to a pile a manure an still smell the sweet grass,
you already in the Lord's favor an standin' in His house.

Quality Time
Isaac Murphy

The first day I showed up in Uncle Eli's barn
he put a shovel in my hand and made me repeat
one Mississippi, two Mississippi, three Mississippi
until I finished shovelin' a stall.

When I started on the next stall, I started the count
all over again. He said he wanted me to do the next
one faster than the one before and that he trusted me
to count Mississippi in my own head.

Everything Uncle Eli said or did—even walkin' the
length of the track each day lookin' for loose fencing,
rocks, gopher holes or anything waitin' to flip the odds
against his hard work—was an important lesson.

Carryin' water buckets and cleanin' stalls every day
made my arms and legs stronger. All those Mississippi's
taught me how to mark time like a clock.

Science Class for Jockeys
Isaac Murphy

Uncle Eli returns from the barrel
we keep outside the barn
and says *this is a horse's breath*
then sets down two full buckets of rainwater.

He says *this is a horse's heart*
and squeezes a little water out of a big wet sponge
he pulls out of a bucket.

Then he wraps a short rope around his fist real tight
and says *this is all the power they legs can hold.*

He says my job is to manage the heart and legs
and lungs, to get to the end with just enough
rope and water to make it across the finish line.

He says *this is the secret to winning a horse race,*
says it ain't no magic or luck—it's science,
and he calls his science *pacing.*

Yardstick

Isaac Murphy

Before I ever got up close to one
I thought they were all legs and tail.

Who'd a thought a horse got elbows
or that inside a hoof is a soft spot

that feels like the heel of my own foot.
Or that I'd make my living

between the withers and the loins.
Who'd a thought that though they measure

the height of a horse in hands
they'd measure *my* five feet in horses?

Groom

Isaac Murphy

The first time I put my hands on a horse
I pretend like I'm touching a woman
or brushing my mamma's hair.

I make sure none of the weight
I might be carrying around
is riding with me.

Before I step foot in a stall
I might even stop   gather myself
in the quiet morning air   close my eyes

and picture my Lucy sleeping
or Mamma peeling apples. It's a lot like prayer,
only I ain't asking for nothing

but for God to lift my burdens
right off of my hands, so that my touch
is like a mother's kiss, like a baptism even.

I just want the horse to know my heart
is clean   to feel all my respect,

no fear, and nothing of the heaviness or darkness
that follow even good men around
like the tail do the mane.

Touch

Lucy Murphy

They say he talks to horses
but I don't know that he needs
to even open his mouth
since he says so much

with his hands. The same way
you hold and massage a baby's fear,
he speaks to his mounts.

Meanness is born of the devil's hands
but, honey, my Isaac's touch
has the power of angel wings.

He lets them know he's not there
to be master. He lets them think
he's just the wind   blowing gently
across their supple necks.

Thy Will Be Done

Lucy Murphy

The *holy* think everything connected
to horses is against God, but my Isaac
says it's clear God made horses to run.

And I say the same God made him
to ride. He don't stand in the infield
and take people's bets.

He don't tell the other horses
to lose. He don't make a man
leave everything he own at the track.

Men who offer money to get him
to throw races soon learn my Isaac
can't be bought for any price.

He rides them horses
as fast as they want to go
and right into the winner's circle.

If he's the best there ever was,
it's God's doing.
Now where's the sin in that?

Perfect Timing
America Burns

They say my Isaac got good timin'.
I reckon that mean
he got a rooster in his head.

He bright enough to know a man's
work begin way before the sun ball
starts climbin' across the sky.

He was lucky enough to find Lucy
who got even better timin' than him.
She own her own laugh.
She filled with her own pluck.

Before we got our freedom
she mighta been carried to Lex'nin
to be sold as a *fancy girl*
instead of bein' Isaac's true love.

She be just that pretty.

'Fancy girl' was a term for female slaves,
usually mulatto, sold as prostitutes
or mistresses to white owners.

Keeper of the Flame

Lucy Murphy

When I first met Isaac
I didn't know a gelding from a broodmare,
but he loved horses so much
I learned to love them too.

I also learned that no matter where a man
gets it, his confidence is a lot like a fire
that has to be tended, stoked and relit
if it ever goes out.

Men work hard to become the legends
they create. But as hard as roosters work
to lift that sun every day, it's hens
that give them something to crow about.

Finer Womanhood
America Burns

My son walk the straight line I drawed,
but a good mirror for daughters
was E. Belle Mitchell from Danville
who I believe could teach a pig to read
if you put one in a schoolroom.

She started out teachin' for the Methodists
out at ol' Camp Nelson.
Them believed they was filled with God
but refused to eat at her same table
before they run her off to Lex'nin.

There be no derbies for colored women.
But if Miss Mitchell was a horse, I'd stand
in line all day just to watch her eat grass.

Come Sunday It's Derby
America Burns

He might not ever tell it to the papers
but I'm the first person Isaac ever see ride.

I'm the first person he watch
get up at dawn
fill a tub wit scaldin' water, soap an dirty clothes

lock everything 'tween my knees
bend over an grab somethin' by its ears
race it up an down the washboard
'til I baptize the dirt right out.

Everybody ride the hell outta somethin'.

I seen a good preacher ride a church full
a people with his words alone, have us
all talkin' back to him while he trot us along
an teach straight from the word a God.

Then once he work up a rhythm
some a us gets up on our feets an urge him on
like our *amens!* is whips
an our *go ahead on, preacher!* is spurs.

Directly he turn a corner an leave the page
an when his tongue starts to gallop
he ride all the way 'til the end a the sermon

'til the whole church is soaked through
with sweat, more exhausted
than any horse an rider I ever seen.

Nomenclature

America Burns

Isaac Murphy's first recorded race was in 1875
under the name Isaac Burns.

We was carryin' Burns, our slave name,
when we first come to Lex'nin.

But I guess it got too heavy for Isaac
once he answered his callin' an needed to be
as free in the saddle as possible.

He tried on my family name
in honor for my daddy, said it fit just fine.
Been callin' himself Isaac Murphy ever since.

Then folks took to callin' him Ike
though I named him Isaac
like Abraham's son in the book a Genesis.

But I guess horse racers an gamblers
ain't comfortable with that much Bible
in they mouths.

Walking Tall
Isaac Murphy

If you told me that I'd wear silk,
that I'd own racehorses and a roomful of books,
that even away from the track I'd be treated
like the tallest man in the room,
I would've thought you'd been kicked in the head.

I've been called names I didn't answer to
but I was never mistreated just because of my size.
Because of racing, I got more respect than most
oak-sized colored men   and I was still a boy.

And even if other riders or unhappy bettors rained
harsh words on my back—if America Burns was
pleased and Lucy Murphy happy, then everybody else
could catch horseshoes in their teeth.

Down the Backstretch

Isaac Murphy

The 1879 Travers Stakes, Saratoga

Aboard Falsetto, the best Uncle Eli-trained colt
I ever rode, my instructions were simply to win.
So we just tagged along for the first mile
and turned the last three quarters into the race.

I learned what he could do a few months back
when he carried me through a mile
like he was toting a bag of feathers,
and I was still holding my winter weight.

Most riders like to sprint right out of the barn
and use the whip until the end of the race.
If my mount will listen, I prefer to hold him back
off the lead but always within striking distance.

I like a horse with enough confidence in his belly
to wait—and legs enough to give me more than
he has left when I ask for it down the stretch.

First Kiss
Isaac Murphy

Kentucky Derby, May 16, 1884

When that chestnut carried me across the line
I didn't know how special it would become.
But like kissing a girl
you always remember the first time.

The track was good. I weighed a dollar and a dime,
sporting Cottrill and Brown's red and white silks.
But I was in no mood to wrestle with Buchanan's
nasty temper—until threatened with suspension.

So at the start of the race the real contest
was between the horse and me. I pulled tight on the reins
to let him know I was not interested in his foolishness.

We were fighting for last place 'til the three-quarter mark.
When he finally surrendered, he put his ears up
and took off like he had extra legs and no rider.

He passed every horse until we pulled ahead in the stretch
and was still there when we crossed the finish line.

I danced with a second Derby aboard Riley and a third
on Kingman   but I will never forget that first kiss.

Mass Choir

Isaac Murphy

The sound of a race is music but like nothing with
strings or words. You'd need a hundred men with
hammers and women stepping Juba but with both
hands making the body a drum   like in 'Hambone.'

Closest thing to it I can imagine would be a whole army
marching in step and singing something like
'The Colored Volunteer' while you listen with your head
inside one of the drums.

Or a large congregation of hands and feet clapping
and stomping together real slow and even in the beginning
and then steadily speeding up but not losing the rhythm

until the whole church is clapping and stomping as fast
as they can and sweat is dripping off their heads and necks
and they all feel like their hearts might bust wide open
but they keep on going faster

and faster and faster   until it feels like God takes over
or a spirit comes down and you are no longer in charge,
just along for the ride.

More Than Luck
Isaac Murphy

I don't pretend to make it sound easy 'cause it's not.
It takes strength, brains and courage,
lightning reflexes and a mountain of confidence.

It takes a jockey's whole body, especially his arms and legs,
to guide that runaway train. Horses have powerful legs
but no muscles below the knees.

So they need great feet and enough training to know
the difference between running free with the herd
and getting a nose across the finish line first.

You've got to be patient and skilled to slip through
the windows and doors that blink open during a race.

But it don't hurt if your horse has already
made up its mind to win
before you ask permission   to climb aboard.

Horseshoes

Isaac Murphy

When I'm up there dodging mud and sprinting
toward the finish line, I don't think about winning.

Don't think the horse does either.
Sometimes I can't even hear the crowd
yelling at me hard and loud
for leading my mount past their first or second choice.

I never consider how easy it is to fall out of the saddle,
how trying to dodge the thunder 'n' lightning

of a thoroughbred's hoofs
would be like tiptoeing through a cotton gin.
When a thousand pounds of horse is on the other end,
your rib cage is just a bird's nest

your head no safer than a watermelon kissing a knife.

Isaacstan

Isaac Murphy

As exercise boys in the barn
we always talked about money,
how little we had of it
and how hard we worked for it.

In the Lodge after many of us
were no longer poor,
our conversations turned
to making our money work
for us and how to enjoy wealth.

After we had enough house and clothes
and my Lucy enough jewels,
I saved and invested in real estate
then started my own stable.

Jockeys wrapped in my red and black silks
made me feel like a man with his own flag.
A man with a flag feels like he owns his own
country. A man who owns his own country
feels like a king.

Black Gentry
Isaac Murphy

I've been to a minstrel show. I know the opinion
some folks have of colored men
and I've seen some of my people believe themselves
to be those same ragged fools.

I don't jig or shuffle. I don't scratch my head
and delight in my own ignorance.

I wear the finest clothes—not to parade around
the Colored Fair, but so strangers know I'm a gentleman.

When they see me traveling with my white valet
from Kentucky to Saratoga to Chicago and back,
they are forced to take pause, forced to look twice.

Mamma taught me that if you want to be treated
with respect you've got to first believe you deserve it.

When people see me without a horse between my legs
I'd rather they look up than down.

I Find It Easy to Deflect
Isaac Murphy

Young and old point at me and their eyes say *hero*.
They probably never heard of Austin Curtis
or other slaves who did more than what I do
a hundred years ago but under the lash.

If I ever saw the 9th or 10th Cavalry,
I'd turn nine again. That many black men
on horseback carrying guns, drawing pay,
still riding high even after the war
would make me turn flips
and chase them through the streets.

I wish they'd point at women
like Mrs. Reynolds who taught me
proper etiquette and how to read and write.

Or ones like my mamma, America Burns,
who carries our people's stories around
on her strong head and neck with more dignity
than I could ever hope to reach for
on my way to the winner's circle.

Negritude Test

Isaac Murphy

Mamma's generation wrestled
with the bear that was slavery
and still carries the scars.

Our fight is with poverty,
a beast almost as vicious.

I have been so successful
at defeating my bear that
many question my blackness.

Accuse me of believing
I am white
or aspire to wake up so.

But if the prerequisite for
owning instead of renting,
wearing suits instead of rags,
eating ham instead of scraps

and enjoying champagne over
pot liquor   is being white,
then I'm as Irish as they come.

Truth Talk

Isaac Murphy

When I am among the gentry, my speech slows enough
to ease between the bones

of every word I offer up to those who would judge
the size of a man's brain by the words at his command.

With Mamma, the only rule when talking is to speak
whatever is on your heart

so we fall quickly into the music I grew up on,
worrying none about putting a bit on our tongues
or being the first one to cross the line.

Looks Like a Rich White Lady, But

Isaac Murphy

When invited as the special guests of owners
or when attending dinner parties thrown in my honor,
Lucy can carry a parasol

pick up the right fork and butter her bread
like any daughter or wife of money.

But her real gift is how she can catch the eyes
of the white-gloved dark-skinned servants

invisible to many in the room,
cakewalk with them across the floor
without even leaving her seat—

sending them back to the kitchen singing
Mrs. Isaac Murphy is one of us.

Oh, Weep No More Today

Isaac Murphy

The head must bow and the back will have to bend,
wherever the darkey may go...
—'My Old Kentucky Home' original lyrics

Seems like every parlor I visit
has one of Foster's plantation melodies
as sung by Christy's Minstrels out on display.

I'm afraid of what it is white folks
hear in that white sheet   music
that gets them so full of tears
when they sing those songs.

They replaced the parts about Poor Uncle Tom
with My Old Kentucky Home.
But it's still about a slave expressing sorrow
for being sold down the river.

It's still about a man separated
from his loved ones, now toiling in sugarcane fields.

I hope what the good in them hears
is a man missing his family and his humble cabin,
that they are not pining for their days
as southern royalty, of being so far up at the top

they couldn't see it was
colored folks in bondage they were standing on.

Silver Stakes
Lucy Murphy

Once when my Isaac was traveling, I polished my silver.
Not some white lady's silver, but my own.

I lined up my gravy ladles, banquet spoons,
asparagus server, salt cellar and pepper grinder
on our dining room table —
and pretended I was trackside at a derby.
I added two big candle holders to fancy up my track.

The salt took off first with the pepper close behind.
Isaac was aboard my favorite spoon—a wedding gift
from my mother—and right on everybody's heels.

I moved the pieces around the table until every piece
was neck and neck. The entire china cabinet cheered
as they galloped down the white linen stretch.

I don't have to tell you which spoon won.

Attitude Adjustment

Isaac Murphy

Our house is filled with monuments to my success,
trophies and tokens of my affection for Lucy.

But when I feel lost in it all or in danger of believing
my own newspaper clippings, we hitch up a carriage

rest our fancy clothes and shoes, pack a basket of food
and ride deep into the countryside

to smell honeysuckle and keep company
with things that really matter.

God's House

Isaac Murphy

We have traveled by train and steamboat
from crowded cities to country towns
and have always slept well anywhere people value
speed, beauty and the excitement of a close race.

I would never complain about any place I could
wake up next to the smell of my Lucy's skin
and the music of a blacksmith's hammer
singing with the birds in the morning.

I own property in Chicago but prefer the fresh air,
clean streams and rolling meadows
we have here at home.

Any horse or lover of horses who dies
and moves on to God's house
would end up back here   in Kentucky.

Empty Nest
Isaac Murphy

When winter quits teasing and finally lets go,
I lie in the dark with my Lucy
way before the sun even thinks about morning

tucked under a quilt like two ears of corn
in the same husk, quiet and listening,
counting how many different songs and voices

we hear singing in the treetop choir outside our window.
These mornings remind her of childhood.
They remind me it's the redbird's mating season.

It will be years before I know this is the closest
we will get to having little voices of our own.

Pound for Pound

Isaac Murphy

Boy riders don't weigh nothing but air.
But once they start eating the chicken 'n' dumplings
of marriage, they start to get meat on they bones.

Lucy was never as good a cook as Mamma,
but even the smell of her biscuits put extra pounds
on me. When they raised the riding weight to 118,
it gave me a few more years in the saddle.

Dropping twenty-five or thirty pounds for a race
is not easy. A man can sweat the first five or ten
exercising in heavy clothes.

Or he might consider burying himself up to his neck
in manure to see if the promise of reduction is true.
I've never been that desperate.

Sometimes we managed our weight by what they call
flipping—chewing up good food, swallowing it,
then pretending that meal was on a string.

It helped me keep my weight down, but seeing me
bent over in a corner made many believe I was a drunk.

Too Heavy

Lucy Murphy

When I won it was all right, but when I lost...
they would say, 'There, that nigger is drunk again.'
—Isaac Murphy

It's all I can do to try to fatten my Isaac
when racing season is over.

He stumbles home mostly skin and bones
and has to relearn how to hold down food
while I try to feed and love him back to life.

But as soon as the hollow in his face and eyes
starts to disappear, the next season comes knocking.

He might nibble on nothing but a biscuit
and coffee the whole long day. I don't know
where he finds the strength to ride.

Some say he took to drinking champagne
as a meal before races after he stumbled off
a losing mount and collapsed.

But I know he nearly starved himself to death
in order to weigh next to nothing
to make the horses think he just a whisper in their ear.

Character

Isaac Murphy

I try to always conduct myself with integrity
during a race. When I believed a fix was on,
I returned the colors and the mount.

Last year during a race, a group of jockeys
all in on a scam planned to cause a spill
with me at the center.

When I figured it out, I unloaded my boot
from its stirrup, kicked the quickly drifting
horse to avoid the collision and moved out
and away from other threats.

I still suffer inside for the pain I caused
that magnificent animal   but I'm sure
the organizers of such foul play
never lost a thimble of sleep.

Blinders
Isaac Murphy

I'm not no two-minute man.
That's just how long it take for my mount
to sprint a mile and a quarter.

I won the Derby at Latonia five times.
Got four American Derby trophies.
I took three at Churchill Downs.

But at least twice a day
somebody called me nigger.

I waited for white folks to look at me
and see a man.

To catch me near a stable
without my racing silks on—
and not want to put a shovel in my hand.

The Power of Sports
Isaac Murphy

Men who might call a colored exercise boy
every foul name they can pronounce
and add more salt by placing dirty or nigger
in front of it

turn around and tip their hats to me
as if everything I do during a race
separates me from my blackness,
making me an honorary white man.

They call me mechanical, stoic and all business
at the track, but riding a horse fast is easy
compared to my toughest job—holding rein
over the large, angry, bitter colored man
that lives inside.

Don't Let the Nigger Win

Isaac Murphy

When white riders still loyal to Confederate ideas
started to show up at the track, it got more dangerous.

Some would kick and punch and use their whips on us
more than their mounts. They would try to run
black riders into the fence or cut us off all together

sometimes knocking our horses to their knees
and us to the ground. But the bloodier racing got,
the crowds got louder and more excited.

Black jockeys paid with their lives or careers
when the race stopped being between horses and silks
and became one between skins.

You can out-think another horse and rider
but if a group of them got it in their minds
to not let you win, it becomes a different game.

Prayer Vigil
America Burns

There be plenty a ways
for the devil to do his work.

Stringin' up a man or burnin'
his house down be almost too easy

when he can cause more mischief
by just bein' a thorn in his side
or findin' ways to make his row longer.

Devil always busy.
So I don't waste no prayers
to keep Isaac off the noose
or out a harm's way.

I don't pray for crooked roads
he travel to be made straight.

I just ask the Lord to always let
the devil an his works be visible to Isaac,
an pray he use his head an heart
to handle the rest.

Ain't Your Uncle Tom or Uncle Remus
Eli Jordan

Durin' slavery times the very best black jockeys
often got mentioned in the racin' papers.
Abe Hawkins was one of the most successful ever.
They just called him Abe or Old Abe

which ain't much different than Uncle
while usin' the whole name of white riders.
But a slave couldn't hardly complain about that.
One name is better than bein' left out altogether.

Or bein' called Master So 'n' So's colored boy
especially when they was already men.

There's somethin' 'bout Uncle in front of a name
instead of Mr. that stings a little, whether it be
in black print or rollin' off white tongues.

Be a shame them believe they
payin' you a compliment
by simply acknowledgin' you exist.

The Color of Racing
Eli Jordan

When they say black jockeys dried up
because they 'started to get too big,'
I say hogwash.

Even before the argument 'tween
the Blue an Gray, most all horse people,
except when it come to ownin',
looked like me.

An why wouldn't they?
It was hard, dangerous, thankless work.
It's still hard, but at least after the war
we could hire our services out
to the highest bidder.

Half a Lexington was colored,
an when we started comin' to the races
with our loud, proud, free selves
they started addin' special seatin' an boxes

so that rich white folks
didn't have to rub elbows
with the same people they used to own.

The same folks who still cooked they food,
washed they clothes an floors,
an watched over they babies.

Between not hirin' blacks, made-up suspensions
an accidents that left many black riders
crippled or dead, I believe somebody
in a back room somewhere made a plan

to keep all the green,
to make horse racin' a whites-only sport.
So they forced us out a the business one by one.

The first Kentucky Derby had thirteen black riders.
A generation later you could hardly find one.

Isaac Grants an Interview
Isaac Murphy

My best day in the saddle was in Detroit
when I won all four of my races.
But most people talk about the duel
between the white rider Snapper Garrison
and me at Sheepshead Bay.

It was a near perfect ride down the stretch.
He tried to run me down in the last quarter
but I kept my pace.

I knew what my horse could do
but hardly anybody was breathing
when we won by a head.

The race made headlines.
People even wrote songs and poems about it.

Later we met head to head
in a match race at Monmouth's track.
I didn't hold back and beat him
by at least four lengths — and allowed
myself a rare public smile.

That was probably my great undoing
for not everybody was pleased with the results.

And not more than a month later when I returned
to the Park aboard the fine Firenze
I could barely keep myself in the saddle.

We placed a miserable seventh in a field of seven.
My critics blamed my poor performance
on too much earlier celebration.
Said I'd gotten too proud.

Only Lucy believed the truth. My body
had been poisoned. My ability to ride suffered.
My reputation fared even worse.

Colored Jockeys Show the Way
New York Herald, September 20, 1889

If a composite photograph had been made
of the jockeys who rode the six winners
at Gravesend yesterday afternoon,
it would have been as black as Erebus.

There wouldn't have been a single light in it,
unless the camera had happened to catch
Hamilton with his mouth wide open,
displaying the pearly white teeth
which form the only relieving feature
on his coal-black face.

The sons of Ham outrode the children of Japheth
with a vengeance, for not a single white boy
was successful in guiding a winner past the judges.

It was a field day for the dusky riders,
and they forced their Caucasian competitors
to take positions in the background.

On the Way to the Pasture
Isaac Murphy

The 1891 Kentucky Derby

Maybe it was dropping the lowest bet from five dollars
to two. Maybe it was the presence of so many
beautiful women. But there was so much excitement
in the air we could feel it way out in the stables.

Whatever it was, that large crowd got to see
colored jockeys win, place and show—
with me aboard Kingman for the victory.

It wasn't my last win but it was the last of me at my best.
After that, I rode fewer winners, tried my hand
at owning and training, even starred in a horse play.

But my best days were behind me and I had to try
to adjust to a life in which a good day didn't include
a ride to the winner's circle.

My body's well wasn't nearly as full as it used to be.
And some of the folks that used to stand in line
for a cool drink of me now lined up to spit.

How to Break a Thoroughbred
Lucy Murphy

My Isaac was happiest on the back
of a horse at the end of a big race.
But when he stopped getting hired
to ride, he felt lost.

He tried owning and training
but without a horse beneath him
it felt like the wind didn't blow.

He would spend whole days at the track
watching others race   and come home
a little smaller each time.

They say it was the flipping.
They say it was the champagne.
They say he could no longer make the weights.
They say he lost the desire to win.

I say they thought he forgot his place.
I say they needed to show us who was boss.

They set out to break his spirit—
but ended up breaking his heart.

February

Lucy Murphy

More than five hundred solemn faces crowded into our home to touch the royal-purple trim on the fine casket modeled after General Grant's. All his Lodge brothers escorted the funeral carriage. There were so many mourners and people standing out in the snow they circled the whole of the African Cemetery. Isaac would've been pleased to know that his fans, the papers and so many of his fellow horsemen had not really forgotten him, though their affection would have been better spent if he had heard their songs and smelled their flowers before he died.

Here Lies...
Isaac Murphy

When the pneumonia rode me from this place
they stabled me in a stall at the African Cemetery.

Years later, my bones almost dust, they dug up
what was left then placed me in the ground
beneath a big monument next to Man o' War.

And if that wasn't respect enough they dug us both up
and buried us again at the Kentucky Horse Park.

I know I'm the only black jockey buried here.
And I know I finally got my name and face in stone.

But they left my Lucy back in the cold hard ground
next to an empty hole without me to share forever with.

Even in death I feel the sting of race and sport,
while I hover at the front doors of the Park—
like a ghost lawn jockey.

Healing Songs
America Burns

They calls 'em spirituals
but what them really are
is every bad thing that happen to each a us
rolled up in a ball a sorrow
an placed in the pit a our stomachs.

When we starts to hum an moan
alls we tryin' to do is lift that ball
an let it rise up our throats.

If we can get it alla way to our tongues
we can almost taste the original sins.

But if we can find the strength
to carry it to the end a the song
what we find waitin'   is peace.

An in case we meet so much darkness
we think can't be no God, He put somebody
in our lives that allow us t'see God
in everything they do. I knowed some dark days
but He sent me Isaac.

Praise Song

Frank X Walker

Straddling the distance between
African Cemetery No. 2
and the Kentucky Horse Park,
between the straw-lined stables
at Churchill Downs
and the view from Millionaires Row,
between our racist history
and our proud past,
I offer these words, this elegy,
this praise song for Isaac.

For every master teacher
blessed with a willing student,
for Jimmy Winkfield and William Walker,
Pat Day and Calvin Borel,
Eddie Arcaro and Angel Cordero Jr.,
for every jockey hypnotized
by the speed, power
and the music of racing.

For every trainer, groom, hot walker
and stable hand who palmed a brush,
carried a bucket or lifted a shovel.

For every Derby Day hero
generous enough to take a jockey
along for the ride,
for every yearling dreaming
of a garland of roses,
for every also-ran.

I recommit this husband to his wife,
this son to his mother,
this student to his teacher.
I offer all of them to each of us.

I dedicate this ride to a man
whose life's work was a blueprint
for anyone   black, white or brown
hoping to build something better,
hoping to fulfill their own potential,
to use all their gifts and blessings
in an honorable way.

Isaac Murphy's life teaches us
how to honor our parents,
how to love full speed,
how to outrun prejudice and oppression.

I dedicate this ride
to America and Kentucky's son,
to a legacy worthy of a star on the walk,
a boulevard named in his honor,
this book.

Wrap your arms around his story,
close your eyes,
feel the wind whispering in your ears.

Grab the reins of any and everything
that makes your heart race.
Find your purpose. Find your purpose.
And hold on.

ACKNOWLEDGMENTS

Earlier drafts of the following poems appeared in
Red Mountain Review, *Appalachian Heritage*, *Motif 2*,
and FishousePoems.org: 'Murphy's Secret,' 'Yardstick,'
'How Faith Works,' 'The Right to Bear Arms,'
'More Than Luck,' 'Come Sunday It's Derby,'
'Silver Stakes,' 'I Thought Slavery Was a Song,'
'Oh, Weep No More Today,' 'Groom,' 'Horseshoes,'
and 'I Dedicate This Ride.'

I am especially grateful to Dr. Anne S. Butler and
the archives at the Center of Excellence for the Study
of Kentucky African Americans at Kentucky State
University. The following books were invaluable:
*Two Minutes To Glory: The Official History of the
Kentucky Derby* by Pamela K. Brodowsky and Tom
Philbin; Edward Hotaling's *The Great Black Jockeys*;
Patsi Trollinger's *Perfect Timing: How Isaac Murphy
Became One of the World's Greatest Jockeys*; and
The Civil War by Geoffrey C. Ward, Kenneth Burns
and Richard Burns; as well as articles from
The Courier-Journal, *The Thoroughbred Record* and
the *Lexington Herald-Leader*; and the documentary
film *Thunder and Reins* directed by Bruce Skinner.

I am also grateful to Hari Jones and the African
American Civil War Memorial and Museum; and
to the following institutions: Lexington Children's
Theatre, Carmichael's Bookstore, the Kentucky Horse
Park, Churchill Downs, Keeneland, Camp Nelson
Civil War Heritage Park, and the Urban Readers
of Louisville; as well as numerous individuals who

provided early motivation, conversation, ears
and eyes on the poems including Toi Derricotte,
Cornelius Eady, Thomas Sayers Ellis, Ed Roberson,
Colleen J. McElroy, Angela Jackson, Nana Lampton,
Filly Tierney, Nicole Bryan, Quiana Townes,
Sherina Rodriguez, Jocelyn Burrell, Nicole Sealey,
Kevin Vaughn, Sheila Carter-Jones, Ciara Miller,
Rickey Laurentiis, the Affrilachian Poets, Larry Snipes,
Bruce Warner, Wanda Reardon, Debra Kinley,
Theresa Smith and Gerald Smith.

And finally, I am most grateful for the skillful
carving and polishing of the original manuscript into
a book and the generosity, attention and tenderness
given to every single word by the editors/designers/
publishers/family at Old Cove Press: Nyoka Hawkins,
Myra Hughes and Gurney Norman.

—*Frank X Walker*